Zodiac Signs

DiscoverRoo
An Imprint of Pop!
popbooksonline.com

VIRGO

by Elizabeth Andrews

WELCOME TO DiscoverRoo!

This book is filled with videos, puzzles, games, and more! Scan the QR codes* while you read, or visit the website below to make this book pop.

popbooksonline.com/virgo

abdobooks.com

Published by Pop!, a division of ABDO, PO Box 398166, Minneapolis, Minnesota 55439.

Printed in the United States of America, North Mankato, Minnesota.

042025
082025

THIS BOOK CONTAINS RECYCLED MATERIALS

Cover Photo: Splendoura Prints; Shutterstock Images
Interior Photos: Getty Images; Shutterstock Images; Wikimedia Commons
Editor: Tyler Gieseke
Series Designer: Laura Graphenteen

Library of Congress Control Number: 2024948393

Publisher's Cataloging-in-Publication Data

Names: Andrews, Elizabeth, author.
Title: Virgo / by Elizabeth Andrews
Description: Minneapolis, Minnesota : Pop!, 2026 | Series: Zodiac signs | Includes online resources and index
Identifiers: ISBN 9781098247973 (lib. bdg.) | ISBN 9781098248512 (ebook)
Subjects: LCSH: Virgo (Astrology)--Juvenile literature. | Virgin (Astrology)--Juvenile literature. | Zodiac--Juvenile literature. | Astrology--Juvenile literature. | Astrology--Charts, diagrams, etc.--Juvenile literature.
Classification: DDC 133.52--dc23

*Scanning QR codes requires a web-enabled smart device with a QR code reader app and a camera.

TABLE OF CONTENTS

CHAPTER 1

MEET THE VIRGO!

Virgo is the sixth sign of the zodiac. People with the Virgo sign are born from August 23 to September 22. When people ask for your "star sign," they are likely asking for your sun sign. This is the zodiac sign the sun appeared in at your birth.

Morning Glory

WATCH A VIDEO HERE!

August 23–September 22

VIRGO

ZODIAC CALENDAR

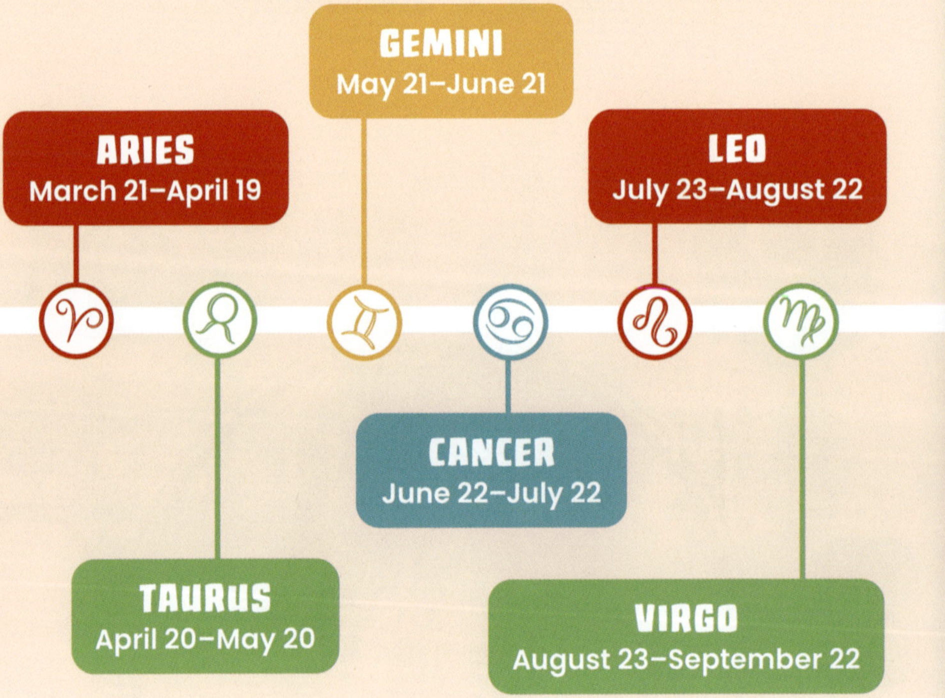

Three features help describe zodiac signs. Signs can be masculine or feminine. Each zodiac sign is given a mode. The three modes are cardinal, fixed, and mutable. Each zodiac is also

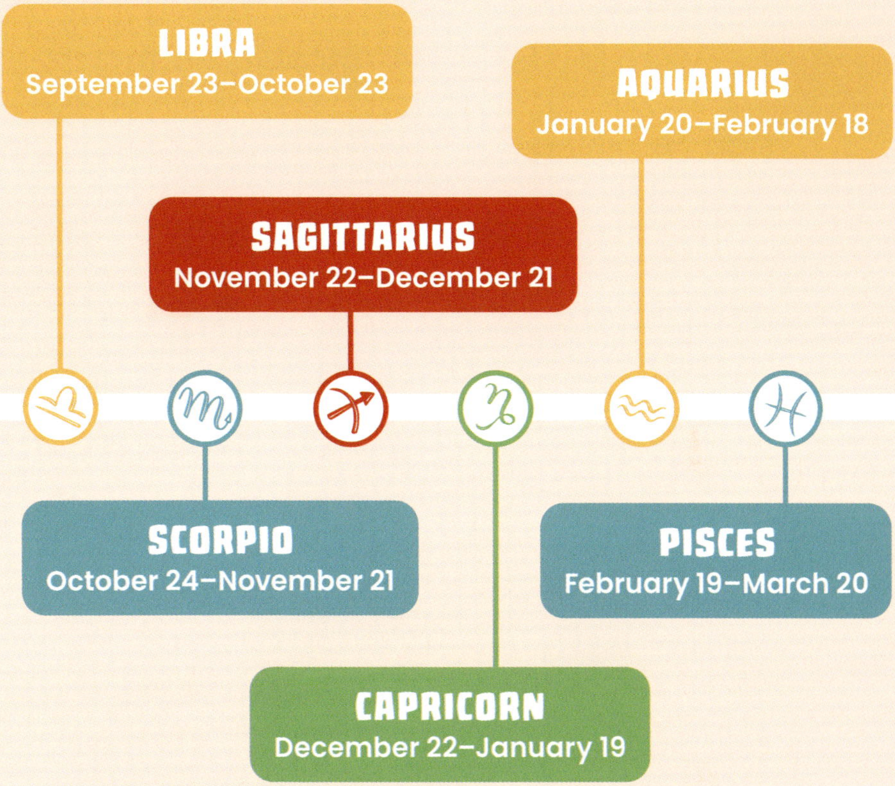

a fire, air, earth, or water sign. No zodiac signs share the same three features.

DID YOU KNOW?

Virgos get along well with water signs.

Virgo is a feminine, mutable, earth sign. Feminine signs are grounded. Many of their actions are done **internally**. They are in touch with their own emotions and those around them.

Nut bearing trees such as the chestnut are connected to the Virgo sign.

Earth signs might enjoy quieter hobbies than fire signs.

Modes describe how signs interact with the outside world. Mutable signs are open-minded and comfortable with change. They are usually easygoing. Earth is the slowest-moving element. Earth signs are often dependable people with lots of plans. They are steady and calm.

Ancient Greeks prayed to Demeter and gave her gifts so their crops would grow.

Virgos are **represented** by a maiden. The maiden was usually a goddess of the harvest. In ancient Greece, the Virgo **constellation** was connected to Demeter, the goddess of the harvest and autumn. It was also connected to Persephone, the queen of the underworld and goddess of spring. Sumerians saw the Virgo constellation as Ishtar, the goddess of war and **fertility**.

Sumerians were a group of people who lived over 5,000 years ago in a region known as Mesopotamia.

CHAPTER 2

HISTORY OF ASTROLOGY

Humans have looked for life's **spiritual** meaning since the beginning of time. They often looked to the stars for this. Astrology is the practice of reading the movements of planets and other **celestial** bodies and connecting them to life on Earth.

LEARN MORE HERE!

Some ancient people used the zodiac signs to predict future events.

Babylonians invented the zodiac in Mesopotamia over 5,000 years ago. Mesopotamia was the first known civilization. Babylon was one of the region's largest cities.

Ptolemy was an Egyptian man who studied the stars.

Earth and our solar system are in the Milky Way galaxy.

The zodiac is a belt of space around Earth that has 12 well-known **constellations**. Ancient people noticed that the sun seemed to move in front of these constellations throughout a year. The sun spends about a month in each constellation.

The constellations in the zodiac belt are Aries, Taurus, Gemini, Cancer, Leo, Virgo, Libra, Scorpius, Sagittarius, Capricornus, Aquarius, and Pisces. Together they make up the 12 zodiac signs. They are all **represented** by different **symbols**.

Islamic astrologers created new ways to map and measure stars.

THE ZODIAC WHEEL

DID YOU KNOW? Most zodiac symbols are animals. The ancient Greeks called the belt of space *zodiakos kyklos,* or "circle of animals."

CHAPTER 3

THE PERFECTIONIST

Virgo is ruled by Mercury. Mercury is the planet of intelligence, communication, and the sharing of ideas. Virgos are known for making good, thought-out decisions. They want their choices to help their friends and the world around them.

EXPLORE LINKS HERE!

Zendaya is a Virgo. She was born September 1, 1996.

Virgos are patient when learning new things.

Virgo is the sign of self-improvement. Virgos often want to prove themselves useful. The person they most often want to prove this to is themselves. Virgos like to learn new skills and subjects. They are interested in anything that can make them helpful to others.

Virgos struggle sitting still. They are hard workers. They do not like to put anything off for tomorrow that could be done today. Virgos are known to set up systems that will help them accomplish things as **efficiently** as possible. They use planners, calendars, and lists.

Virgos like to have a schedule and plan. It makes them feel comfortable.

As earth signs, Virgos enjoy the outdoors. They love to plan a trip.

The Virgo drive for success often makes them fear failure. They are good at noticing things. People count on the Virgos in their lives to bring order to **chaos**. Virgos can look at problems, see where things are going wrong, and then put everything back together in better order.

Sapphire is the stone of wisdom and loyalty.

DID YOU KNOW?

Virgos are reserved. They don't want attention on themselves when they succeed.

CHAPTER 4

THE HELPING HAND

Virgos are smart. They have good memories and can think clearly. Virgos do not make any decisions without thinking them through. They like to study and find out all the facts when facing problems or choices. Sometimes, Virgos can be excitable. They react quickly and with great emotion.

COMPLETE AN ACTIVITY HERE!

Virgos often have a few very close friends.

Virgos love deeply. However, they are slow to get close to people. They may be this way because they struggle getting in touch with their own emotions. Virgos are happy to dig deep on exciting subjects and projects, but they do not like doing that **internally**.

DID YOU KNOW? Virgos can be too honest with their thoughts. They might hurt their friends' feelings.

When Virgos get close to people, they are kind and go above and beyond to help their friends. They are the friends that can be counted on to get things

The city of Istanbul in Turkey is connected to Virgos. Virgos may enjoy it there!

done. People go to Virgos when they need advice. Their judgment can be trusted on anything from business decisions to the best movies and music!

Virgos need to care for themselves too. Their mental and physical well-being are very connected. If they get overpowered by thoughts and projects, they often feel sick. Staying active and eating **nourishing** foods help Virgos stay healthy and balanced in their mind and body.

The Virgo constellation can be seen in the Northern Hemisphere between spring and summer. It can be seen in the Southern Hemisphere between autumn and winter.

Today, astrology can answer questions about an individual. People use astrology to understand who they are and why they might do what they do. It can also help people understand others in their life. A zodiac sign can point out personal skills, possibilities, and internal **motivations**.

WHAT IS A BIRTH CHART?

Each person's birth chart contains all the planets in our solar system, the moon, and the sun. The location of where each **celestial** body was based on the exact time and location of a person's birth can be marked on a birth chart. A birth chart can explain even more about a person than what only a sun sign can. The placement of each planet affects the drive of a person. This reveals personal motivations. Astrology experts can read birth charts.

MAKING CONNECTIONS

TEXT-TO-SELF

Are you a Virgo? If so, do you think the sign matches your personality? If not, what do you have in common with Virgos?

TEXT-TO-TEXT

Have you read any books about the other zodiac signs? How were those signs similar to and different from Virgo?

TEXT-TO-WORLD

With the help of an adult, look up famous Virgos. Pick one person and write a few sentences about ways that person shows Virgo qualities.

GLOSSARY

celestial — having to do with the sky or outer space.

chaos — a state of utter confusion.

constellation — a group of stars that forms a pattern.

efficiently — working in a way that gets results, with little wasted effort.

fertility — the quality of being able to create life.

internal — of, relating to, or being on the inside.

motivation — something that makes one want to do something.

nourishing — helping to grow or improve.

represent — to stand for or be a sign of.

spiritual — having to do with people's beliefs in things such as the soul, nature, and what happens after death.

symbol — an object or picture that represents something else.

DiscoverRoo!
ONLINE RESOURCES

This book is filled with videos, puzzles, games, and more! Scan the QR codes* while you read, or visit the website below to make this book pop.

popbooksonline.com/virgo

*Scanning QR codes requires a web-enabled smart device with a QR code reader app and a camera.